POCKET RUPAUL

WISDOM

WITTY QUOTES & WISE WORDS
FROM A DRAG SUPERSTAR

POCKET RUPAUL WISDOM

WITTY QUOTES & WISE WORDS
FROM A DRAG SUPERSTAR

Hardie Grant

BOOKS

CONTENTS

RUPAUL ON...

LOVE

'LOVE DRAG, LOVE QUEENS, LOVE PEOPLE WHO DANCE TO THEIR OWN DRUM.'

VARIETY
17TH AUGUST 2016

'IF YOU CAN'T LOVE
YOURSELF, HOW
IN THE HELL YOU GONNA
LOVE SOMEBODY ELSE?'

RUPAUL'S DRAG RACE,
SEASON 1 EPISODE 1

'MAKE LOVE. LOVE PEOPLE.
BE SWEET. HAVE CORN
DOGS. DANCE. LIVE. LOVE.
FUCK SHIT UP.'

VULTURE
23RD MARCH 2016

'IF YOU'RE GORGEOUS-LOOKING ACCORDING TO *VOGUE* MAGAZINE AND YOU HAVE AN EVIL HEART, THAT MAKES YOU REALLY UGLY IN MY BOOK… CONTRARY TO POPULAR BELIEF, A GORGEOUS HEART AND SOUL WILL TAKE YOU FURTHER THAN GOOD LOOKS.'

CREAM
AUGUST 1994

'I THINK THAT SWEETNESS
AND KINDNESS ARE
AT THE TOP OF MY LIST
OF HUMAN VIRTUES.'

DAZED
21ST SEPTEMBER 2016

'AS GAY PEOPLE,
WE GET TO CHOOSE
OUR FAMILY.'

RUPAUL'S DRAG RACE,
SEASON 5 EPISODE 7

'IN A CULTURE, YOU CAN CHOOSE FEAR OR LOVE.'

METRO WEEKLY
7TH APRIL 2016

'I LOVE TO LAUGH, I LOVE COLOUR, I LOVE TEXTURE, AND I LOVE CREATIVITY.'

INTERVIEW
9TH MARCH 2013

'NOTHING IS REAL, EXCEPT PERHAPS LOVE.'

THE STAR
30TH JUNE 2016

'EVERYBODY SAY LOVE!'

GAY TIMES
JULY 1993

RUPAUL ON...

DRAG

'DRAG IS REALLY ABOUT MOCKING IDENTITY. DRAG IS REALLY ABOUT REMINDING PEOPLE THAT YOU ARE MORE THAN YOU THINK YOU ARE – YOU ARE MORE THAN WHAT IT SAYS ON YOUR PASSPORT.'

DAZED
1ST JUNE 2015

'DOING DRAG IN A MALE-
DOMINANT CULTURE
IS AN ACT OF TREASON.
IT'S THE MOST PUNK-ROCK
THING YOU CAN DO.'

ROLLING STONE
4TH OCTOBER 2013

'INHERENT IN DRAG
IS THAT WE'RE MAKING
FUN OF EVERYTHING,
WE'RE WINKING LEFT AND
RIGHT AT EVERYTHING.'

SPIN
1ST APRIL 2013

'DRAG AIN'T FOR SISSIES. YOU'VE GOT TO TOUGHEN UP.'

ABC

12TH MAY 2016

'DRAG HAS ALWAYS BEEN PUNK ROCK BECAUSE IT CHALLENGES IDENTITY.'

METRO
7TH APRIL 2016

'ALL OF US HERE ON THIS PLANET, WE ARE GOD IN DRAG.'

IDOLATOR
5TH MAY 2014

'ALL THINGS TO DO WITH
DRAG ARE INHERENTLY
THERAPEUTIC... YOU HAVE
TO GO INTO THIS COMPLETE
ARTIFICE TO FIGURE OUT
WHO YOU REALLY ARE.'

ROLLING STONE
4TH OCTOBER

'DRAG QUEENS ARE LIKE THE MARINES OF THE LGBT MOVEMENT. WE SUIT UP, WE SHOW UP, AND WE'RE ALWAYS READY TO SERVE.'

METRO WEEKLY
7TH APRIL 2016

'EGO LOVES IDENTITY.
DRAG MOCKS IDENTITY.
EGO HATES DRAG.'

PINK NEWS
8TH AUGUST 2011

'I THINK THE STORY
OF DRAG REALLY HAS
TO DO WITH NOT TAKING
LIFE SO SERIOUSLY.'

MOVIELINE
1ST FEBRUARY 2010

'DRAG SAYS "LOOK,
I'M A MAN, NOW I'M A WOMAN,
NOW I'M A COWBOY, NOW
I'M A SAILOR." IT'S ALL
ABOUT SHAPE SHIFTING.'

IDOLATOR
5TH MAY 2014

'DRAG WILL ALWAYS EXIST BECAUSE IT IS REALLY AN ENLIGHTENED STATE.'

CURVE
20TH JANUARY 2009

'DRAG DOESN'T COVER WHO YOU ARE, IT REVEALS WHO YOU ARE.'

ATTITUDE
7TH JULY 2015

'THIS IS PROBABLY THE GOLDEN AGE OF DRAG RIGHT NOW.'

VOGUE
2ND MARCH 2015

'ANYBODY WHO CAN STEP OUT OF THE HOUSE WITH A PAIR OF HIGH HEELS AND SOME LIPSTICK ON THEIR LIPS IS MY HERO.'

ODYSSEY
14TH DECEMBER 2015

'THROUGHOUT THE HISTORY
OF THE GAY RIGHTS
MOVEMENT, DRAG QUEENS
HAVE ALWAYS BEEN
AT THE FOREFRONT.
WE THREW THE FIRST
BRICK AT STONEWALL.'

WASHINGTON POST
24TH AUGUST 2016

'WHEN YOU BECOME A
SHAPESHIFTER, WHEN YOU
CHOOSE TO LIVE A LIFE SO
CONTRARY TO WHAT SOCIETY
TELLS YOU TO DO, YOU BECOME
A WALKING TESTAMENT
TO THE OTHER SIDE.'

GUARDIAN
3RD JUNE 2015

'[DRAG] ACTUALLY DIDN'T SAVE MY LIFE, IT GAVE ME A LIFE.'

VULTURE
23RD MARCH 2016

RUPAUL ON...

HERSELF

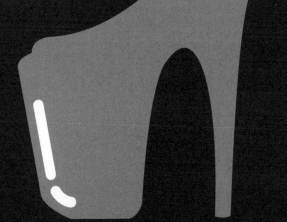

'AT FIVE YEARS OLD, I REALIZED I WAS A SUPERSTAR TRAPPED IN A FIVE-YEAR-OLD'S BODY. AND I HAD TO DO SOMETHING ABOUT THAT!'

WASHINGTON POST
17TH SEPTEMBER 1993

'[I TAKE THE ROLE OF] THE SHAMAN, OR THE WITCH DOCTORS, AND THE COURT JESTER WHOSE JOB IT IS TO REMIND THE CULTURE: THIS IS ALL FACADE. DON'T TAKE IT TOO SERIOUSLY.'

ROLLING STONE
4TH OCTOBER 2013

'OH, DON'T GET IT TWISTED —
I'M LIKE AN OLD PROSTITUTE.
AS LONG AS THEY'RE WRITING
CHEQUES, I WILL BE THERE!'

VARIETY
17TH AUGUST 2016

'I HAD A STALKER WITH MY NAME TATTOOED ON ONE LEG AND SHE HAD CHER'S NAME ON THE OTHER LEG SO I WAS IN GOOD COMPANY.'

VICE
17TH OCTOBER 2016

'MY MOTHER WAS MY FIRST INSPIRATION; SHE WAS TOTALLY A DRAG QUEEN.'

WASHINGTON POST
17TH SEPTEMBER 1993

'WHATEVER OTHER PEOPLE THINK OF ME IS NONE OF MY BUSINESS.'

LA TIMES
10TH AUGUST 2016

'I COME FROM A LONG LINE OF PEOPLE WHO IDENTIFY AS FREAKS, FREAKS OF NATURE, WHO QUESTION EVERYTHING AND DECIDE, "I'M NOT GONNA PUT A LABEL ON IT. I'M JUST GONNA GO FOR IT."'

THE ADVOCATE
24TH AUGUST 2016

'I MOVED HERE WITH JUST
A PAIR OF HIGH HEELS
AND A DREAM... AND LOOK
AT THE BITCH NOW.'

GAY TIMES
JULY 1993

'I'D RATHER HAVE AN ENEMA THAN HAVE AN EMMY.'

VULTURE
23RD MARCH 2016

'IN ALL THESE YEARS THAT
RUPAUL HAS BEEN RUPAUL,
THERE'S BEEN NO BITCH WHO
HAS COME FOR THIS CROWN.'

NPR
25TH AUGUST 2016

'I ALWAYS FELT LIKE THE LITTLE BOY WHO FELL TO EARTH AND SO, THE CLOTHES, THE COLOURS, THE MUSIC, THE SOUNDS, THE TASTES, THE SMELLS — ALL OF IT WAS SOMETHING I WANTED TO EXPLORE AS A HUMAN ON THE PLANET.'

THE STAR
30TH JUNE 2016

'MY IMAGE IS TWO PARTS DIANA ROSS AND CHER, ONE PART DAVID BOWIE AND THREE PARTS DOLLY PARTON.'

DAZED
21ST SEPTEMBER 2016

'WITH HAIR, HEELS AND ATTITUDE, I'M THROUGH THE GODDAMNED ROOF!'

GAY TIMES
JULY 1993

'LOOK AT ME – I'M A BIG OLD BLACK MAN UNDER ALL OF THIS MAKE-UP, AND IF I CAN LOOK BEAUTIFUL, SO CAN YOU.'

THE ADVOCATE
3RD OCTOBER 1995

'I AM VERY AMAZED AT HOW THINGS HAVE TURNED OUT FOR ME, ESPECIALLY GIVEN WE ARE A PRIMITIVE CULTURE ON THIS PLANET, AND THE THINGS I'VE BEEN ABLE TO DO ARE SO PROVOCATIVE THAT IT AMAZES ME.'

THE PRESS AND JOURNAL
9TH FEBRUARY 2016

'I AM A GIANT "FUCK YOU" TO BIGOTRY. BUDDHA, KRISHNA, JESUS, AND NOW RUPAUL.'

THE ADVOCATE
23RD AUGUST 1994

RUPAUL ON...
CULTURE

'MAINSTREAM CULTURE HAS ALWAYS CO-OPTED GAY CULTURE OR SUBCULTURES; OUR VERNACULAR, OUR FASHION, OUR LANGUAGE. BUT GUESS WHAT? WE'VE GOT WAY MORE WHERE THAT CAME FROM. WE'RE STILL 10 YEARS AHEAD OF THE CURVE.'

GUARDIAN
3RD JUNE 2015

'THE ONLY PERSON WHO INTERESTS ME IN POP CULTURE RIGHT NOW IS JUDGE JUDY.'

VULTURE
23RD MARCH 2016

'ANYONE WHO SAYS IT'S AN HONOUR JUST TO BE NOMINATED IS ONE LYING BITCH.'

RUPAUL'S DRAG RACE
SEASON 7 EPISODE 5

'IMPERSONATING BEYONCÉ IS NOT YOUR DESTINY, CHILD.'

NPR
10TH JUNE 2011

'WHETHER YOU'RE DRESSED UP TO BE WORKING ON WALL STREET OR WORKING AT MCDONALD'S, WE'RE ALL DRESSING UP.'

THE STAR
30TH JUNE 2016

'EVERY TIME I BAT MY FALSE EYELASHES IT'S A POLITICAL STATEMENT.'

NPR
10TH JUNE 2011

'BY CHANGING MY OWN MIND, THE WORLD CHANGED.'

INTERVIEW
9TH MARCH 2013

'KNOW THYSELF, KNOW YOUR HISTORY, AND KNOW HOW TO READ THE LANDSCAPE.'

VOGUE
2ND MARCH 2015

'READING IS FUNDAMENTAL.'

RUPAUL'S DRAG RACE
SEASON 2 EPISODE 7

'WHEN YOU'RE FAMOUS, PEOPLE SCRUTINISE EVERY INCH OF YOUR CHARISMA, UNIQUENESS, NERVE AND TALENT.'

RUPAUL'S DRAG RACE
SEASON 6 EPISODE 4

RUPAUL ON...
LIFE

'DON'T LET PEOPLE OR SOCIETY OR YOUR IDEA OF YOURSELF KEEP YOU FROM LIVING THIS LIFE AND ENJOYING ALL THIS LIFE HAS TO OFFER.'

MOVIELINE
1ST FEBRUARY 2010

'ENJOY IT NOW, BUY YOU A SYNTHETIC WIG, GET YOU A PAIR OF CHA-CHA HEELS, GET YOUR DRIVER'S LICENSE, AND HIT THE ROAD, BABY.'

IN CONVERSATION WITH
PAUL HOLDENGRÄBER
20TH MARCH 2015

'RISE UP AND BE FEARLESS, LIKE A MASAI WARRIOR. STAKE YOUR CLAIM IN THIS LIFETIME.'

TODAY
29TH JANUARY 2010

**'GOOD LUCK,
AND DON'T
FUCK IT UP.'**

RUPAUL'S DRAG RACE
SEASON 1 EPISODE 1

'YOU GO OUT THERE AND YOU KNOCK THEM DEAD, BECAUSE YOU ARE A WINNER, BABY!'

IN CONVERSATION WITH
PAUL HOLDENGRÄBER
20TH MARCH 2015

'IF AT FIRST YOU DON'T SUCCEED, BECOME A LEGEND, HUNTY!'

RUPAUL'S DRAG RACE ALL STARS
SEASON 1 EPISODE 1

'I REALLY DON'T CARE
HOW HISTORY REMEMBERS
ME – I WON'T BE HERE.
I NEED TO MAKE TODAY,
THIS MOMENT, THE MOST
FABULOUS MOMENT EVER.'

VICE
25TH AUGUST 2016

'NOW GO FORTH, AND BE SICKENING.'

RUPAUL'S DRAG RACE
SEASON 4 TEASER

'YOU HAVE TO GO OUT THERE AND OWN WHAT IT MEANS TO BE A BADASS BITCH.'

GUARDIAN
3RD JUNE 2015

'REMEMBER WHO YOU REALLY ARE. UNLEASH THE DRAGON AND LET THESE BITCHES HAVE IT!'

TODAY
29TH JANUARY 2010

'IF YOU PAY ATTENTION
TO YOUR HEART AND NOT
WHAT OTHER PEOPLE SAY,
YOU PROBABLY WILL HAVE
A REALLY GOOD TIME HERE
ON THIS PLANET.'

THE PRESS AND JOURNAL
9TH FEBRUARY 2016

'I THINK INSTEAD OF GIVING KIDS A DIPLOMA AFTER SCHOOL, I WOULD GIVE THEM A WIG AND A PAIR OF HEELS AND SAY, "GIRL, GO LIVE, GO DISCOVER YOURSELF."'

CREAM
AUGUST 1994

'IF I NEED COLOUR AND SYNTHETIC HAIR OR ACRYLIC NAILS OR FLARED PANTS OR A HIGH-HEELED SHOE, THEN SO BE IT! THAT'S THE ONLY WAY I CAN SUSTAIN MYSELF IN THIS HIDEOUS, HORRENDOUS, MEDIOCRE WORLD.'

DAZED
21ST SEPTEMBER 2016

'ALL THESE OTHER SONS
OF BITCHES ARE TAKING
IT ALL TOO SERIOUSLY.'

DAZED
21ST SEPTEMBER 2016

'IF YOU DON'T HAVE
A SENSE OF HUMOUR
ABOUT YOURSELF, YOU
ARE FOOLING YOURSELF.'

VOGUE
2ND MARCH 2015

'MY MISSION STATEMENT IS: I CAME TO THIS PLANET TO HAVE A GREAT TIME, HAVE FUN, MEET PEOPLE, DO FUN THINGS.'

VICE
25TH AUGUST 2016

'ONCE YOU GET OFF THAT
STAGE, SEE YOURSELF AS
A CONSTRUCT, THEN YOU CAN
HAVE A PARTY, THAT'S WHEN
YOU CAN HAVE SOME FUN.'

IN CONVERSATION WITH
PAUL HOLDENGRÄBER
20TH MARCH 2015

'YOU HAVE TO BE BEAUTY *AND* THE BEAST, YOU HAVE TO BE BERRY GORDY *AND* DIANA ROSS, YOU HAVE TO BE SONNY *AND* CHER, DO YOU FOLLOW?'

IN CONVERSATION WITH
PAUL HOLDENGRÄBER
20TH MARCH 2015

'USE ALL THE COLOURS, TOUCH ALL THE TOYS AND LICK ALL THE CANDY! DO IT ALL.'

VICE

25TH AUGUST 2016

'I DON'T CARE IF YOU ARE IN
THE BACKSEAT OF A TRICK'S
CAR, OR IF YOU'RE IN CHURCH,
OR IF YOU'RE ON STAGE.
DO *NOT* TAKE YOUR SHOES OFF,
DO *NOT* TAKE YOUR WIG OFF.'

BUZZFEED
7TH MARCH 2016

'OBVIOUSLY, I PREFER JOY
OVER PAIN BUT WHAT I HAVE
TO SAY IS SOME OF MY MOST
PAINFUL EXPERIENCES HAVE
BEEN THE MOST EDUCATIONAL.'

TRANSFORMATION 50
2005

'HANDLE YOUR SHIT, LADYKINS, AND BE PREPARED.'

IN CONVERSATION
WITH DAVID ATLANTA
1ST APRIL 2014

'THE ONLY WAY TO GET THROUGH IT IS TO LAUGH AT IT.'

THE AV CLUB
24TH JANUARY 2011

'DON'T BE SORRY.
BE FIERCE.'

'NEVER STAY SMALL TO TRY TO FIT IN. YOU WERE MEANT TO STAND OUT. YOU WERE MEANT TO BE A STAR.'

ATTITUDE
APRIL 2015

'SASHAY AWAY.'

RUPAUL'S DRAG RACE
SEASON 1 EPISODE 1

POCKET RUPAUL WISDOM

FIRST PUBLISHED IN 2017 BY HARDIE GRANT BOOKS, AN IMPRINT
OF HARDIE GRANT PUBLISHING

HARDIE GRANT BOOKS (UK)
5TH & 6TH FLOORS
52–54 SOUTHWARK STREET
LONDON SE1 1UN

HARDIE GRANT BOOKS (AUSTRALIA)
GROUND FLOOR, BUILDING 1
658 CHURCH STREET
MELBOURNE, VIC 3121

HARDIEGRANTBOOKS.COM

BRITISH LIBRARY CATALOGUING-IN-PUBLICATION DATA.
A CATALOGUE RECORD FOR THIS BOOK IS AVAILABLE
FROM THE BRITISH LIBRARY.

ISBN: 978-1-78488-128-3

PUBLISHER: KATE POLLARD
SENIOR EDITOR: KAJAL MISTRY
EDITORIAL ASSISTANT: HANNAH ROBERTS
PUBLISHING ASSISTANT: EILA PURVIS
ART DIRECTION: CLAIRE WARNER STUDIO
COVER ILLUSTRATION © MICHELE ROSENTHAL,
WWW.MICHELEROSENTHAL.COM
IMAGES ON PAGES 7 © MAXIM KULIKOV, 19 © LAYMIK,
39 © DELLUXO, 57 © ALMA HOFFMANN, 69 © VALERY,
ALL FROM THE NOUN PROJECT
COLOUR REPRODUCTION BY P2D
PRINTED AND BOUND IN CHINA BY LEO PAPER GROUP